WINTER IS YOUR BEST SEASON

HOW TO MAKE THE MOST OF LIFE'S DIFFICULT SEASONS

P. A. PENNANT

All Scripture quotations are from the King James version,
New King James version and the Amplified version.

Shining Light Publishing
ISBN 978-0-9549788-2-2

Introduction

In the winter of 1993 I found myself alone, pacing about my large bedroom, screaming at God and asking the question, "Why?"

"Why were you doing this?" I can hear you asking. What happened? Well, my beloved mum had sadly died in the January of that year and my eldest sister passed in September of the same year. It felt all too much… so by the month of November, although comforted by the relevant promises in the bible; I still needed some answers to my unanswered questions. It was then in my moments of despair and emotional turmoil, that I heard the Lord respond to me and say, "Stop asking why and ask what?" I retorted with impatience and anger, raising my voice, I shouted the word "What?"

The Lord now had my undivided attention so I stopped pacing and slumped onto the nearby bed. Perched on the edge of the firm mattress, I sat up and listened and as I did so the Lord began to show me images of the four seasons,

Spring, Summer, Autumn and Winter. This was the beginning of perhaps one of my greatest life lessons, one that has helped me through the changing scenes of my life. He revealed to me that life is about seasons and that at some point these seasons of life on earth must come to an end. My mother and sister's times and seasons of life were complete and whist reflecting on these times, I began to understand and appreciate that it is the quality of life that matters most not the quantity.

"it is the quality of life that matters most not the quantity."

It is this life lesson about seasons that I am about to share with you as we observe and explore the seasons and discover their meaning, purpose and application for our lives.

May your perspective on your life never be the same again!

Contents

Chapter 1:
Spring

The Book of Genesis is the book of beginnings and therefore is the best place to start our journey. Genesis records that in Noah's lifetime God set seasons in place after the destruction of the earth by the rain He had promised. Noah and his family were the only survivors and I believe it was a consolation to them that as long as planet earth exists God promised that there will be four seasons; spring, summer, seed time and harvest.[1] It would not rain forever and there would never be a flood as devastating as Noah and his family experienced ever again.

[1] Genesis 8:22

For the purpose of this discourse, whilst I am aware that seasons vary in time and temperature across our globe; I will focus on the seasons we are familiar with in the United Kingdom.

Spring can be considered to be the first season because it is a season of new life just as it was in the beginning of the world. Everything was new. We will address it as the first season, a season of new things, new beginnings.

Spring is the transition time between Winter and Summer. It symbolises the concepts of rebirth, renewal and regrowth.

In springtime daylight lasts so much longer than in Winter as the sun shines equally on the north and south. The first day of Spring marks the warming up of the earth following the colder temperatures of Winter. Spring is the lambing season, a time when millions of new lambs are born.

Spring also signals the return of birds that have hibernated during the winter, who welcome the season with their songs. In addition the month of April onwards presents an ideal time to plant seeds in preparation for a harvest in the succeeding months. Flowers bloom and trees begin to bud and blossom as the season progresses. King Solomon who could be considered one of the wisest men in the Scriptures spoke of this change of seasons in the Songs of Solomon.[2]

"The flowers are springing up the season of singing birds has come and the cooing of turtle doves fills the air"

[2] Song of Solomon 2:12

Recognising your Spring season

You know when you are in a spring season because like the birds responding to the warmer temperatures you can sense your spirit beginning to lift… to warm up and sing again after a long winter. You sense internal change and a change in your external atmosphere.

You know when it's Spring because you feel expectant as identified in my previous description of Spring. There's a feeling of newness, new beginnings, new opportunities, new ways of thinking. It's a time where you feel ready to take on fresh information and adopt a positive and progressive mindset. You will recognise and embrace new experiences and open doors ahead and consequently you will make new decisions that will create the future and impact you desired and aspire to achieve.

'Spring ushers in new creative ways to approach life and relationships.'

You'll identify an eagerness to learn again, to take a decisive hold of life and to face the challenges you encounter with hope and optimism.

Spring speaks of untapped potential, the new frontiers yet to be discovered and conquered.

It ushers in new creative ways to approach life and relationships. It presents the option to attempt what once required effort and do it effortlessly because the season enables the impossible to become possible.

What to do in your Spring

- Enjoy and welcome the freshness of this season.
- Embrace the new.
- Hope again. Dream again.
- Make plans.
- Embark on a new course, career, job or relationship/s
- Connect with a new group/ network.
- Attempt to do the things you have desired and always wanted to do.

Chapter 2:

Summer

Seasons were created by God. They are not created to be static but to be ever changing cycles. They are not designed to last forever.

We have identified that Spring time is a time for new things; therefore, we must be willing to prepare for the new and in practical terms that often requires change.

One of the most immediate changes that is required in response to seasons is a change of clothing. During sunny Spring days and certainly during the Summer season many people readily don their T shirts, shorts and sandals in order to welcome the sun to radiate and tan their bodies.

Summer is perhaps often the most awaited and definitely the most popular season. Why? Because it's the warmest season that falls between Spring and Autumn, during the months of June, July and August.

At the summer solstice, the beginning of Summer, the days are longest and the nights are shortest, with day-length decreasing as the season continues.

Summer can be a season of extremes i.e. sunshine, flooding due to rainfall or destructive drought. At best one can enjoy the baking heat waves of a Summer's day, at worst one can experience heavy rainfall, or so much sunshine that drought kicks in. Consequently, lush green grass can become dry and burnt and plants and animals needing to be refreshed due to dehydration.

Summer can be a colourful season as the sunlight magnifies the brightest of colours of flowers and vegetation. Trees and flowers are fragrant and in full bloom. Beautiful, attractive insects fill the air with incredible sights and sounds. Trees and bushes drip with ripe sweet tasting fruit and berries.

Summer is a time to holiday, relax and unwind. It's a season to enjoy, with so many taking vacations at the seaside or in a sun soaked holiday resort at home or abroad. For many, summer holidays provide the well earned rest or break after they have been working so hard throughout the first half of the year.

Recognising your Summer season

So how do you know it's Summer for you? You know you're in Summer because it feels like it's the time of your life. Everything is just beautiful, relationships, life, the world. What could possibly go wrong?

You know you're in Summer because you just sense you are at a peak. You've reached a summit... the fullness of all that you are encountering in life at that time.

In Summer, we seek to make the most of the weather and want to be in the best of health and wealth.

Despite this we know that Summer can be blighted by drought and therefore during Summer despite the changing circumstances, we have to decide to prosper and succeed. We have to decide to make the most of and get the best out of all situations.

'You know you're in Summer because you just sense you are at a peak. You've reached a summit'

What to do in your Summer

- Relax and unwind.
- Enjoy a time to rest.
- Enjoy the best that God-gives you in life, in terms of work, food, exercise, health and relationships.
- John the apostle, said to early believers I wish that you may prosper and be in health even as your soul

prospers.[3] I believe for us to prosper or progress, for things to go well on our way, we must monitor and maximise our thoughts, our emotions and our choices. As our thoughts feelings and will line up with God's Word and His Spirit[4], we can decide to prosper and be certain of success.

This principle of success is presented to Joshua[5] and King David who reiterate this truth in the Psalms[6]. Both biblical references speak of the value of meditating, speaking out and obeying the Scriptures in order to progress or succeed. We must renew our thinking with the Word of God in order to experience real change.[7]

- Our thoughts determine our behaviours, so it is important that during the spring and summer seasons of our lives that we let go of old mindsets and embrace new ones. We need to be willing to change because we understand that it's not going to be Summer all year round, as much as we may like it to be. Life inevitably has its highs and lows, its peaks and its troughs, its sun and its rains.
- Use the time of rest to be refreshed and rejuvenated for the months ahead.

---

[3] 1 John 3:2

[4] Proverbs 16:3 AMP

[5] Joshua 1:7-9

[6] Psalms 1:1,2

[7] Romans 12:1-2

- Avoid becoming too comfortable. Summer can be without doubt the most enjoyable season, however, all good summers come to an end so it is vital not to become too comfortable as becoming too comfortable can bring about stagnation and prevent essential progress.

Chapter 3:
Autumn

King Solomon reminds us in the book of Ecclesiastes[8] that there is a time for every purpose under the sun, a point of view which is concurred by the prophet Daniel.[9] It is not a new principle but one that is established in the book of Genesis where God institutes the seasons of seed time and harvest, summer and winter.

Having journeyed though from Spring to Summer, we now arrive in Autumn. We have acknowledged that Spring is a season for new things and a time for new beginnings. Summer is a time of full bloom and prosperity, the season

---

[8] Ecclesiastes 3:1

[9] Daniel 1:12

that once completed at the end of August, leads us to this season of further significant change: Autumn or the 'fall'... the fall of leaves as identified in the Americas.

Autumn can be considered a very beautiful season in that the rich spectrum of the vivid greens of summer make way for the vibrant yellows, reds, oranges and browns of Autumn as the chlorophyll and the greenery the leaves once held is no longer present.

Trees which were once fully clothed in thick green foliage begin to undress gracefully exposing their sturdy skeletal frames by which they stand and grow year by year. This process provides protection and conservation for the next season. In Winter, trees take in sufficient water through their roots. In this way the tree can conserve water and stay alive. If the autumn leaves remained water would escape as water vapour through the tiny pores in the leaves. Towards the end of Autumn, fruits and nuts are harvested and the days become shorter and colder as the temperature declines in preparation for Winter.

'Setbacks are often set ups'

Recognising your Autumn season

You can recognise that you are in an Autumn because it will be evident that things/ situations are changing in our lives. Items and relationships we once held onto appear to be slipping away or indeed falling away. Certain friends may no longer call. There may be loss of a job or finances/ resources and opportunities begin to 'dry up'. It may include the loss of health, a job, career and sadly the loss of a loved one.

Autumn is a season for us to let things go and appreciate what remains, We need to allow the birds to take their songs with them so that they can return with new songs.

We must also remember that God is setting us up. Setbacks are often set ups. The apostle Paul makes it very clear that. 'All things work together for the good of those who love God and called for His purposes as stated in Romans 8 verse 28. So despite difficulties and changes around us, God is working things out for our benefit.

'People are like trees'

Autumn facilitates exposure of what is already present. It helps you to see what things and people are like in their vulnerable state. People are like trees. Trees can be 'dressed ' or 'undressed' and like trees we have our basic structure. It's evident that difficult circumstances expose our true characters and reveal what our values and beliefs truly are.

What to do in your Autumn season

- Let it go!! Paul formerly known as Saul of Tarsus said all he counted gain he counts as loss[10]. Whatever you give up or let go for Christ's sake in this life you'll gain in this life and the next. Let go of the old so that the new can come. Throw out or give away old clothes

[10] Philippians 3:1-14

and old shoes and items. Release old habits and all that is unnecessary. We must remember that who and what served us today may have a completely different purpose tomorrow. With the help of Holy Spirit identify and let go of every weight or sin that easily hinders your progress so that you can move forward without restriction.

- Autumn is the ideal time to reflect and hunker down in preparation for the Winter as things are likely to get worse before they get better.
- Don't compare yourself with any one else. Appreciate and value yourself. Like trees we are all different. We are who we are by the grace of God!
- Autumn presents the opportunity for us to move out of the familiar and comfort zones to possess all God has for us.

Chapter 4:

Winter Is Your Best Season

Finally we arrive at the season which many may consider to be the worst ...Winter...Why? Because it's often a wet, cold and dark time. It's a time to visit our wardrobes yet again and have another change of clothing from the minimum to the maximum; we wrap up warm to face inclement weather.

We've identified that Spring is a time for new things and new beginnings. Summer is a time of fullness and prosperity. Autumn can be a beautiful season and a time of change, a time to let go of the old to make way for the new.

Winter is without doubt the coldest season of the year often characterized by cold weather, ice and snow. Snow silently falls and covers the ground, leaving a soft white blanket. Snow often makes short appearances during winter and sleds and snowmen along with snowball fights attend for fleeting episodes lasting a few days or less. Snow has its drawbacks in that it can bring life to a halt during a heavy fall as it creates the potential to close down whole cities, towns and nations and ultimately leave sludge filled streets.

Despite all of this, snow has its benefits, it can insulate the soil and in doing so protect bulbs and roots ensuring they are preserved for regrowth. Winter has health benefits too; it encourages us to make the effort to warm up our bodies and as a result we may burn calories. Research has proven that the cold temperature enables us to think more clearly and get better sleep. The season may also help us to reduce allergies and inflammation.

Regardless of the apparent barrenness of Winter, there are still some flowers that bloom and evergreens or coniferous trees remain consistent. It is interesting to note that these trees do not lose their needles and because the needles are narrow and covered with wax, little water escapes from them.

Furthermore, the birds which welcomed the Spring and gloated and glided in the warmth of summer, now migrate to warmer climates. Winter is also a time for hibernation for the animals who need to sleep during this cold season.

In Winter it is important to prepare for the long nights and short days as the earth turns away from the Sun. As a result of long dark nights and these short days, many may become depressed due to low light levels and experience what has come to be known as Seasonal Affective Disorder.

Recognising your Winter season

It can be dark and cold naturally, emotionally and spiritually; nothing seems to be working.

The silent screams one muzzles, suppress internal thoughts and self talk such as 'get me out of here' ' I don't need this right now,' 'Why me?' As with my story, you may be screaming 'Why?' God knows what you can handle and He certainly won't allow you to be overcome by your circumstances or to deal with more than you can cope with.

Winter is a season to settle down, wrap up and stay warm. It's a time of incubation. It can seem long. especially when one experiences difficult times. Just like the sun rotates around the earth and creates darkness, it can seem like God is distant and has turned His face away from us. It can seem as though your situation or circumstances are being overlooked but they are not.

Winter is symbolic of a time of death which will eventually lead to resurrection. Things will get worse before they get better!

To conclude: Winter provides opportunities to rest and a time to incubate.

'Winter is a season to settle down, wrap up and stay warm. It's a time of incubation'

What to do in your Winter season

- Rest.
- Recognise that you are being tested.
- Tests reveal who we are and bring out our characters.
- A young man in the scriptures called Joseph was a prime example of this. Having been rejected by his brothers, falsely accused and imprisoned; he arose from the winter of his life into his Spring, where he was promoted to the role of Prime Minister of Egypt. The apostle James explains this principle so well in that he affirms that we must work through the trials and tests of our faith so that our character can be formed.[11]
- Reflect on all that you have learned in previous seasons.
- Allow yourself to be healed from hurts and pains received in former seasons.
- Insulate: Don't be afraid of aloneness or isolation; they are ideal times to get to know oneself better and ultimately get closer to and develop your relationship with God.
- Winter is a time of rest. A time to rebuild, to recoup to restructure internally in preparation for the new. It's a time to lay low and allow roots to grow deep in time for your Spring. It's a time like a caterpillar in its cocoon to redevelop your strength.

---

[11] Psalm 105:18-20 James 1:2-4

'What occurs internally is simply incredible'

When I reflect on the experience that The Lord Jesus Christ showed me many years ago, I'm reminded that it is the quality of one's life that matters, not the quantity. It is vital to know and understand seasons of our lives and as a result we will be able to maximise them.

The Scriptures speak of us being transformed by the renewing of our minds[12]. In other words there needs to be a reprogramming. The word used for transformation in the original language is the word metamorphoo from which derives the word metamorphosis, as in the change that a caterpillar experiences.

The change of the caterpillar to a butterfly is symbolic of the cyclical seasons we will all experience throughout our lifetime.

The change of the caterpillar to a butterfly is symbolic of the transformation that takes place when a caterpillar transforms from an ugly creature to a beautiful butterfly. It also represents for me, the cyclical seasons we will all experience throughout our lifetime.

Autumn speaks of a time of change. This metamorphosis of the butterfly typifies the process of embracing change and moving from the old to the new. During this time caterpillars eat so that they can grow and shed their

---

[12] Romans 12:1-3.

skins as they grow. Similarly, Autumn is a great time to release the old and take in new information to facilitate growth and development.

Winter The pupa stage is an amazing stage of a butterfly's life. When a caterpillar is fully grown in terms of length and weight it transforms into a pupa or chrysalis. Externally, it appears as if the caterpillar is in decline, however, inside the pupa the business of transformation is swiftly occurring. As in Winter this is a season for transformation,

What occurs internally is simply incredible. From a short crumpled body to immaculate wings and limbs and organs; a beautiful butterfly prepares to emerge ready for the final stage of its life cycle.

Spring When the emerging butterfly appears its wings are soft and folded against its body because it has had to accommodate all its new parts inside the chrysalis. As in Spring it's a time of new beginnings as it appears to fly.

Summer Following a time of rest the butterfly's wings are empowered with blood flow before they begin to flap and fly. In a matter of hours the butterfly experiences the joy and freedom of flying and is prepared for its next stage of reproduction as an adult. I understand that at this stage of their lives adult butterflies seek to reproduce and thus begin to create a life cycle that will start again.

...the future is bright and can only get better.
The best is yet to come.

We must recognise the seasons of our lives so that we don't miss them and respond out of season.

Winter is indeed our best season because it is when things are tough that we are forced to get bitter or better. In order to get better we must embrace difficulty and hardship because God is using trials in our lives to perfect His nature within us. Once we embrace our Winter we will be set up and equipped for all the other seasons. Life becomes an adventure and a welcome challenge because we realise that whatever our circumstances are they must come to an end. Our seasons of life may not be limited with regards to natural seasons, to a matter of three months at a time, however no matter how long your winter is or how dark your night is... the morning has to break!. Spring has to come according to the promise of God.[13]

May you move forward with confidence and understanding, knowing that the future is bright and can only get better. The best is yet to come.

---

[13] Psalm 30:5

Reflection and Application

Questions to answer and action to take

- What season am I in?
- What do I need to do now?
- How can I prepare for my next season?
- What do I need to change?
- How can I apply what I've learned and understood to maximise my life and enable others to make a difference in their lives?

About The Author

P. A. Pennant is a husband, father, an ordained minister, a qualified and experienced teacher of over twenty years and a musician/ songwriter with a passion to bring solutions to people's lives through biblical principles. He has authored three books to date, including: 'Songs for collective worship' for children aged 4-11 years and along with 'Winter is your best Season', 'Church: What is the point?' which presents a biblical perspective and understanding of what church is all about. All books are available for purchase on Amazon by e-book or paperback.

Contact the author by:

Email: slsolutions2019@gmail.com

Facebook: Peter A. Pennant

Instagram: petera.pennant

YouTube: Kairos

Shining Light Publishing

Printed in Great Britain
by Amazon

17789212R00020